SKIING
BASICS

USING THE T-BAR
TO GET UP A HILL.

SKIING BASICS

by
Al Marozzi

Introduction by
Morten Lund
Author and Contributing Editor to Ski Magazine

Illustrated by
Bill Gow

Photographs
Courtesy of
Camelback Ski Area

Edited and Produced by
Arvid Knudsen

PRENTICE-HALL, INC.
Englewood Cliffs, New Jersey

Dedication

To Marilyn Hertz who gave me the opportunity
to put my ski program into practice.

And to my wife, Sandra, and my children,
Chris, Gina and Tricia, with thanks for
their patience.

Acknowledgment

My very special thanks to Robert Gillen
for his skillful editorial guidance and
assistance.

Book Design by Arvid Knudsen

Printed in United States of America   J

Prentice-Hall International, Inc., London
Prentice-Hall of Australia, Pty. Ltd., North Sydney
Prentice-Hall of Canada, Ltd., Toronto
Prentice-Hall of India Private Ltd., New Delhi
Prentice-Hall of Japan, Inc., Tokyo
Prentice-Hall of Southeast Asia Pte. Ltd., Singapore
Whitehall Books Limited, Wellington, New Zealand

10 9 8 7 6 5 4 3 2 1

**LIBRARY OF CONGRESS CATALOGING
IN PUBLICATION DATA**

Marozzi, Alfred.
  Skiing basics.

  SUMMARY: Text and illustrations introduce basic
skiing techniques and equipment.
  1. Skis and skiing — Juvenile literature.
[1. Skis and skiing] I. Title.
GV854.M3145   796.93   80-23650
ISBN 0-13-812289-X

CONTENTS

INTRODUCTION

The most important thing about teaching yourself is to keep from making yourself feel you *have* to do something.

Once you get the feeling that you have to learn to ski, then skiing becomes like to many other things, just something that you must get through, must learn. And that is not the idea of skiing.

Skiing is something you do for the fun of it.

If it's not fun, then it's not skiing.

It's work.

So, how do you make skiing fun?

First, you get somebody who is a good teacher to either teach you or write a book. Al Marozzi is a good teacher. And he has written a good book.

It's good because it tells you a few things, first of all, that you need to know to be comfortable, such as buying skis and ski clothes.

Then he tells you how to get on the skis, climb the hill, and find out things, rather than *do* things. It's not important what you do, exactly. What is important is what you find out for yourself.

Those are the things that you remember.

And the more things you find out, the more you remember, the more easily you can handle your skis on the hill. And pretty soon when you have discovered enough things, you discover that you have learned to ski.

The other way, *making* yourself do certain things, such as making yourself stand up straight and making yourself turn the skis is slower: you find that, the next time out, you have to "learn" all over again. Because when you force yourself to do something, you are also resisting doing it. And the resistance tends to make you "forget."

Look at what happens, for instance, when you find a new toy of some kind: let's say it happens to be a small heavy steel ball. You first roll it on the floor, to see how far it goes. Then you bounce it off the wall, to see how it bounces. Then you spin it on itself to see how it spins. All the while you are discovering things about the ball, you are really finding out how to "handle" the ball. Pretty soon you will be rolling the ball around in the palm of your hand, then on the back of your hand: you're already making the ball do tricks, and haven't even tried to learn anything!

That's the way skiing is learned.

The more you discover and the less you force yourself to do something very specific, the more fun it is, and the more quickly you learn, without having to make skiing into "work."

That is called "the movement theory of physical education," if you want to put a name on it. This is the way gymnastics is taught in many good schools today.

Al Marozzi, who knows an awful lot about teaching physical education through movement, has now written down how to do the same kind of learning in skiing.

It works.

Morten Lund,
Contributing Editor, Ski Magazine

1

Why Skiing Is
So Much Fun

Have you ever had a dream in which you're flying? What a great feeling—soaring among the clouds, high over your friends, your home, or your neighborhood. Well, skiing is like that. Skiing is like jumping off a mountain and the snow cradling your fall. You can turn or speed or glide along until you reach the bottom. Of course then you have to go back up the mountain again. But that's a small bit of work for so much fun coming down.

I think skiing is a great sport. It's easier to learn than you think. You can begin skiing when you're young—six- or seven- or even three-years old—and you can keep skiing until you're eighty-five. That means skiing is something the whole family can do together. Skiing is a sport in which it makes no difference if you're short or tall, fat or skinny. You can ski by yourself or in a group. You can ski all day and even at night in some places.

If you're good, you can race. Many areas offer races every weekend for beginning to advanced skiers. Perhaps you saw some ski racers on television during the Olympics—with a lot of hard work you might be able to be there yourself eight or twelve years from now. If you like working outdoors you could become a ski instructor some day. Or you might like to work as a ski patroller, a person who keeps the mountains safe, is an expert in first aid, and helps skiers who get into trouble.

Skiing can help you improve your balance and coordination, especially how you position your body when you move and how you control your feet. Bicycle riding, dribbling a soccer ball, and running around tacklers with a football are all sports that demand good balance and coordination. Perhaps you already know how to roller skate, ice skate, or how to ride a skateboard. If so, learning to ski will be a snap. Surfing and waterskiing are helpful, too, if you're lucky enough to have had the chance to try these things.

But even if you haven't tried a lot of sports, you *can* learn to ski.

2

Getting Outfitted

There are three ways to get outfitted for skiing:
      (1) *You can rent.*
      (2) *You can borrow, or*
      (3) *You can buy equipment.*

Renting Equipment

I recommend that you rent equipment for your first few ski trips. Ski shops, ski areas, and small shops close to ski areas offer quality equipment at reasonable half-day to weekly rates.

Renting is often a good idea because trained people help to fit you properly and the equipment is up to date and reliable. Be sure to tell the rental shop people that you are a beginning skier—don't exaggerate—so that they can fit you correctly and safely.

Borrowing Equipment

Borrowing someone else's equipment is inviting trouble. Unless the person is exactly your size and at approximately your level of ability, the equipment won't fit you properly. And even if it *seems* to fit, how do you know for sure that it's right for you?

When you borrow equipment, it is always a good idea to have a ski shop check over the boots, skis, and bindings before you go skiing. Even though it may cost you $10 or $15 to have the gear checked, it is money well spent, because faulty, badly fitting gear can result in serious injury if you take a bad fall.

Buying Equipment

It's great to have your own equipment, but be careful. Don't buy the cheapest skis, boots, and bindings you can find. Since your body changes rapidly as you grow, until you are about seventeen-years old, you will outgrow equipment long before you wear it out. Many people buy their gear at "swap" sales, which are sponsored by ski clubs, shops, schools, and church organizations. You can save 40 to 50 percent of the cost of good, new equipment by buying slightly used gear at a swap sale.

To learn about these swap sales, watch your local newspaper or ask the nearest ski shop for information. One item you will grow out of most quickly is ski boots. It's a good idea to swap for larger-size ski boots every season. Meanwhile, you can get several years of use from a good quality set of skis and bindings.

Whether shopping at swap sales or buying from a retail shop, it makes sense to bring along an adult who is an experienced skier to help you make a selection. Salespeople should know a lot about choosing the right equipment, and you should ask them plenty of questions. If they don't seem to have the answers, try another ski shop. And don't feel you have to buy from the first store you visit.

You can't learn too much about ski equipment. Read about equipment in the ski magazines, and be very honest about your ability and experience when talking to salespeople. Find out what kind of maintenance is necessary to keep your equipment in tip-top shape.

What You Need

Skiing equipment includes skis, boots, bindings (which fasten the boots to the skis), poles, ski runaway straps (sometimes called "safety straps") or ski brakes, and warm clothing.

Skis

Ski manufacturing has improved so much in the last few years that there are many, many good skis to buy. Most skis are made of a combination of materials, often using wood combined with fiberglass on the inside and on the outside aluminum. A beginning skier should look for a ski than turns easily—this usually means a ski that is "flexible"—and one that is steady through the bumps and grips the snow and ice well with its steel edges. Generally, a beginning skier will want a flexible ski that is a little shorter than average so that the ski will be easy to control while the skier is learning simple turns.

SKIS FOR BEGINNERS SHOULD
BE ABOUT EYE-HEIGHT.

A good length for a beginning skier is a ski that reaches from the floor to between the shoulder and the head. The following chart shows sample ski lengths for various heights.

(feet, inches)	(centimeters)	(feet, inches)	(centimeters)
3'7"	110	4'11"	150
3'9"	115	5'1"	155
3'11"	120	5'3"	160
4'1"	125	5'5"	165
4'3"	130	5'7"	170
4'5"	135	5'9"	175
4'7"	140	5'11"	180
4'9"	145	6'1"	185

Variations in individual ski designs may indicate that a particular ski should be purchased in a slightly longer or shorter length. Experienced ski shop salespeople can help you pinpoint the correct length.

Bindings

A binding is the piece of equipment that holds the boot to the ski. That may not sound too important, but it is very important. When you fall, it is the job of the binding to "release" the ski from your boot so that strain is not placed on your foot, ankle, or leg. Most broken bones in skiing result from bindings that have not done their job properly.

There are three basic types of bindings: *turntable bindings, step-in bindings,* which are usually easier to use, and *plate bindings,* which are often best with used boots. One brand of binding automatically snaps the ski back onto your foot after it releases, and this is very convenient. But it is also more expensive.

Always have your bindings checked by a good ski shop mechanic at least once at the start of each season. Check your bindings frequently yourself, and watch for free binding checks by the National Ski Patrol at ski areas. You can't be too safe.

PLATE BINDING

Boots

Between the ages of eight and thirteen, you will probably have to replace your boots every year. Don't buy boots that are too big! Growing into big boots can be painful and cold and can ruin skiing for you.

Do buy boots that fit snugly around the ankle and comfortably around the rest of your foot. Your toes should be free to wiggle, and when you lean forward, your heel should be held tightly enough so that it does not rise up.

There are two basic types of ski boots: *front entry* and *rear entry*. Almost all modern boots are made of tough, stiff plastic, with molded foam insides, and two, three, four, or five steel buckles to close and tighten them. Choice among top-quality brands is strictly a matter of preference.

When buying a boot be sure to wear the same socks that you will wear when skiing. Often, two pair of socks are worn, although this isn't necessary for warmth with the modern foam-lined boots. The inner sock should be lighter, perhaps made of cotton to allow the perspiration to pass through, and the outer sock should be heavier, usually wool, which keeps the heat in. It is important to keep your feet dry when skiing.

When shopping for boots, try on as many as possible to get the best possible fit. Your feet control your skis through the boots, and if the fit isn't exact, you have no control. When buckling the boots be sure that they are neither too tight nor too loose. The buckle that is over the area of your foot where shoe laces would be should be the tightest. The buckle over your toes should be loose enough to allow your toes to wiggle. The top buckles should be secure enough to keep the upper part of the boot snug against your leg.

Poles

The ski pole is used for balance and for precision in making turns. It is composed of a *shaft, grip,* and *basket.* The length depends on your height. Turn the pole upside down, and grasp the pole above the basket with your arm bent at the elbow. The correct length for you is a little higher than your hips. Poles should be light and maneuverable.

15

Pole grips come in two styles: *grips with straps and those without*. When gripping poles with straps, place your hand through the strap from underneath, holding the strap and the handle. When using poles with strapless grips, be aware that there are a right pole and a left pole. Check the groove on the grip where your thumb would go; this will help you find the right side.

Ski Straps or Brakes

The ski "runaway strap" keeps your ski from shooting off down the hill after your binding releases during a fall.

Sometimes, though, in a fall where a skier is really flipped around, the ski itself, attached by the strap, can whirl around and hurt the skier. Thus ski brakes were invented. Ski brakes stop runaway skis by digging into the snow with a "brake" that is activated after the binding releases. The ski will only slide a short distance from the skier before coming to a complete stop.

In some ways ski brakes are safer than safety straps. However, many areas require safety straps for those who ride on chairlifts, even if skiers already have ski brakes, in case a ski releases while the skier is up in the air. Also, safety straps are less expensive than ski brakes.

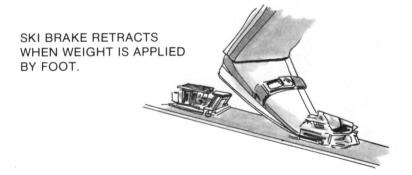

SKI BRAKE RETRACTS
WHEN WEIGHT IS APPLIED
BY FOOT.

The Right Clothing

Warmth, comfort, and ease of movement are the requirements of ski clothing and you needn't be a millionaire to dress for the sport.

16

Hat

Wear one—a warm one. Cover your ears.

Ski Mittens

Ski mittens keep your hands warmer than gloves. Good mittens should have tough leather exteriors and be waterproof and warm.

Ski Pants

Insulated bib overalls are great, particularly for cold days on the chairlift, but a modest prices pair of jeans over thermal underwear can do the trick just fine. Have a dry cleaner give your ski jeans a water-resistant treatment.

Jacket

A ski jacket should be water and wind resistant and insulated. A light, insulated jacket, backed up with several layers of turtleneck, shirt, and sweater, is much more practical. If it gets a little warmer, you can always peel off a layer.

Goggles

Goggles aren't absolutely necessary, but they're very handy. Treat them carefully.

3

Learning to Ski

Alpine

In the first two chapters, we have been referring to "downhill skiing," which is also called Alpine skiing. There is also "cross-country skiing," which is called Nordic. These two types of skiing have key differences. Downhill is just what the name says: skiing downhill. It is fast and thrilling, and ski lifts are used to haul skiers back up the hill to save time and energy (and this is why you buy a ski-lift ticket at ski areas).

Cross Country

Cross country is skiing trails without lifts—across the flats and up and down hills. Cross-country skis are lighter, narrower, and have less of an edge than downhill skis. Cross-country boots are soft and flexible, and bindings allow the heel to lift easily off the ski. This lets a cross-country skier "run" on his skis, and some experts refer to cross-country skiing as running, for that reason. Special ski bottoms and precise use of waxing allow a cross-country ski to grip the snow and not slide backwards when the skier pushes off on the ski.

Many people enjoy cross-country skiing like they do jogging. It's great exercise and it's a nice, quiet way to enjoy the woods and back country. It costs less than downhill skiing. The equipment is much less expensive and trail fees on public courses are often as low as $2 or $3—sometimes there's no charge at all. Compare this to full-day lift ticket prices of $10 to $18 at downhill ski areas (going to $20 now at several major ski areas).

Although there are technical differences between the two types of skiing, practicing either teaches balance and coordination, which is immediately helpful to doing both. Many cross-country skiers are using their lighter equipment at downhill areas, combining many of the advantages of both types of skiing. If you have a lot of snow in your area, but very few hills, cross country can be an excellent way to begin skiing at the lowest possible cost. This is a sport that can be very demanding—so take your time getting used to the equipment, and rest as you get tired.

19

CROSS-COUNTRY SKIING.

Finding Someone to Teach You

The best way to learn to ski is to do exactly what you are doing right now: Read as much about the sport as possible.

After you learn some of the basic terms and become familiar with different equipment, you should definitely try to take lessons at a certified ski school. When you first start skiing, short series of lessons will correctly teach you all the basics. You can keep practicing those basic skills for years, getting better and better. Learning by yourself will give you a lot of bad habits that you will have to unlearn, and this is more difficult and takes up more time (and more ski-lesson money) than taking the lessons when you first start to ski.

Following are some of the ways you can get help in learning to ski.

Physical Education Classes

Ask your gym teacher about giving some ski instruction, even if it's only an introduction.

Joining a Ski Club

Join a ski club at your school. If your school doesn't offer one, suggest that one be started (how to do this is covered later). If for some reason it isn't possible at your school, check with your church, with local boy scout and girl scout organizations, with the YMCA and the YWCA, and with your city's recreation department. It is very likely that one group or another offers ski-club activities. Joining a club will give you the benefits of getting much cheaper rates and of making new friends who have the same interests as you.

Ski Schools

Most ski areas have ski schools that will take you through a series of lessons from beginner to advanced skills. Many schools offer learn-to-ski packages of lessons—a series of lessons over a short period of time at an inexpensive rate. Naturally, ski areas are interested in developing new skiers because new skiers are their future customers. Contact the ski-school director at a local area by letter or phone in order to check out the programs, offered. Good areas will be happy to help you get started as a skier. A good place to find out about local ski areas is in ski shops which often keep pamphlets about the areas on hand. Collect all the brochures and pamphlets you can and compare lesson packages.

Friends

It's great to have a good friend who is a skier and who is willing to teach you all about skiing, but it's not a great idea to take him up on his offer.

How to Start a Ski Club

If enough of your friends are interested in a skiing activity, school officials should be cooperative about starting a club. Here are some simple steps to get a club going:

21

A SERIES OF LESSONS FROM QUALIFIED
INSTRUCTORS IS ONE OF THE BEST WAYS
TO LEARN TO SKI.

1. *Have people sign a list which states that they are interested in skiing and would like to form a club at school.*
2. *Present this list to the principal and request that a ski club be formed.*
3. *Find out if any of your teachers are skiers and ask them if they would act as advisors to such a club.*
4. *Have a meeting at school about forming the club and announce your discovery in home rooms, in the school bulletin, in the school newspaper, and with posters in order to interest your fellow students.*

Ski Club Activities

Once a club has been formed, there is a lot that can be done. Here are a few suggestions to get things going:

1. *Invite a local ski shop to send someone to a meeting to talk about the latest equipment and, clothing and how to care for them.*

2. *Invite any ski areas within driving distance to give talks about skiing and about their areas. Some areas, in cooperation with ski shops, have terrific movie and slide shows that really show how exciting skiing can be.*

3. *Send away for copies of ski films. Some of these films are free, and others are rented for a small fee.*

4. *Set up a program for beginning ski lessons at a local ski area. This may be arranged as part of the ski area's presentation to your club meeting.*

5. *Plan and arrange a weekend ski trip at a large ski area. A sizable ski club can arrange a sizable discount in skiing and lodging. This trip could be the highlight of the year for you and your friends.*

Learning Without Snow

What happens if you want to learn to ski and there is no snow or you live in a city where you can't easily get to a ski area?

What you *can* do is convince your physical education teacher to include skiing in your gym class.

This was the kind of problem I had while teaching skiing at one particular school. The school had no equipment, and we had to stay inside. Thus, no snow! I solved this problem by working to collect ski equipment with local ski areas, ski shops, and interested parents, making sure that the equipment was safe for beginners. The big step was to design a small slope to be used indoors.

The surface of the ramp is covered with indoor-outdoor carpet, which works well with regular ski bottoms. Every basic skiing skill can be taught and practiced on the ramp.

THE SKI RAMP — A GREAT WAY TO
LEARN THE BASICS OF SKIING WITHOUT SNOW.

Photo courtesy of Al Marozzi

23

Parachute Classes

One device already used by physical education classes and which works well in skiing instruction is a parachute. I have used it in games to introduce beginning skiers to the basic things they need to know to ski. You may wish to suggest this to your physical education teacher. Interest in more ski instruction and a small, snowy hill are all that are needed to conduct outdoor classes. The skills that are taught are walking, skating, stopping, side stepping, step turns, unweighting, traversing, and centering over the skis. These are the things we are about to learn. (Look at the photo to see how the students grab on to the parachute.)

4

Learning the Basics

The best way to start skiing is to take a series of beginning lessons. However, there are basic skills in skiing that you can work on out on the snow at the ski area by yourself, before you enroll for formal ski lessons.

I teach beginners a method that leads to skiing parallel—having the skis together. Other teaching methods stress using wedge or snowplow techniques for beginners—the skis are apart with the tips held in toward each other. I believe that children actually learn to ski parallel more quickly than adults since children are more flexible, more agile, and less tense than older people.

I present each skill three different ways. First, my class tries to discover as much as possible about the skill we are trying to learn. Then we play a game using the skill being taught. Finally, we review everything we have learned, breaking the skill down into understandable parts. You can do this on your own.

Standing and Walking on Skis

Discovery

1. *In how many different directions can you walk with your skis?*
2. *Can you walk with your skis close together? Far apart? Which feels best? Can you feel your skis slide in the snow?*
3. *Can you walk strongly and forcefully with your skis? Can you pound them into the snow and make believe you're squashing bugs?*
4. *In how many different directions can you walk very quietly with your skis on?*
5. *Can you speed up and slow down very gradually while walking with your skis on?*

Game: Follow the Leader

Directions: Use an area that is flat with various obstacles to go around. Find a friend or two and pick a leader. The leader walks through the area doing as many different things on skis as he can. The followers do everything the leader does.

Review: Standing/Walking

(Note: This will be the only time you will use ski poles until you become more advanced.)

1. *Since we have already discovered the most comfortable position to stand in on skis, get into that position.*
2. *Use your poles for balance by slanting them into the snow at your sides.*
3. *Slide the right ski forward on the snow and plant the left pole ahead of your body. Now slide the left ski forward and plant the right pole ahead. Push off with your poles with each sliding motion and try to move along the snow as smoothly as possible.*

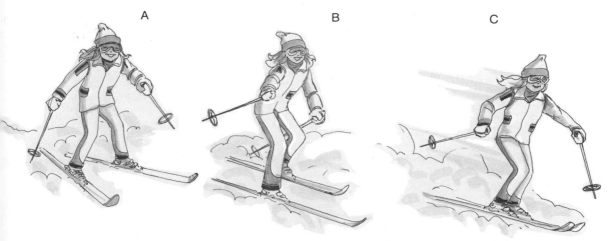

A   B   C

JUST LIKE ICE-SKATING, PUSH AND GLIDE.

Skating

As you get used to walking on your skis, you will want to move faster. To do this, you can skate along the snow with your skis—the same sort of motion you use to move along on ice skates and roller skates.

Skating on skis isn't too difficult, but it takes practice. Find a very slight hill, and begin as if you were going to walk down the slope. Instead of keeping your skis pointed straight down the slope, point the tip of one ski away from your body. Bend your knees slightly, and push off on the snow with the ski pointed out. (Use the inside edge of the ski to push, cutting into the snow with it.) At the same time, slide along on the other ski. Alternate pushing and sliding skis, shifting your balance to the ski on which you are sliding with each push.

Practice skating often, as it is an excellent way to move along on flat areas to save time and energy and will be of great help to you as you get better.

Photograph by Arlene Avril
for Camelback Ski Area

Falling and Getting Up

Discovery

1. *How many different ways can you fall? Which type of fall is the easiest for you to control your body?*
2. *Once you're on the ground, see how many different ways you can find to get back up again.*
3. *Try getting up to one side, to the other side, to the front, and to the back. Which way is easiest for you?*
4. *Try falling and getting up on a steeper hill. Now which methods of getting up are easiest?*

Game: First Up

Directions: Do this on a flat area or slight hill. Have a few of your friends lay down on the snow and be very still for a moment. When you yell "Up!" everyone tries to stand up as quickly as they can. Whoever stands up first wins.

Review: Falling/Getting Up

If none of the ways you have tried to get up seem to work well for you, try this one: Lie flat on your stomach with your feet spread wide apart, skis spread to either side. Slowly push yourself up to a standing position, starting off as if you were doing a push-up, but continuing to push and straighten up.

A

B

C

THE EASIEST WAY TO GET UP.

D

29

SIDE STEPPING

Side Stepping

Sooner or later you will have to climb a slope to get to where you wish to be on a ski hill. Side stepping is one way to do it.

Discovery

1. *How many ways can you move sideways with your skis on?*
2. *Find a small hill, and stand at the bottom with your skis pointed across the hill's slope. Keeping your skis parallel to each other, move to a higher level and then stop. What must your ankles do to keep from sliding back down the hill? What must your knees do to keep you from sliding?*
3. *Can you step up the slope with very strong, forceful movement? With very light, gentle movements?*
4. *Can you side step up the slope very slowly, like a slow-motion movie?*
5. *How fast can you side step up the slope?*

Game: Hill Race

Directions: Start at the bottom of a small hill with several of your friends. Get ready to begin side stepping up. One person yells "Go!" and everyone tries to step up to the top of the hill as quickly as possible. First person to the top wins.

Review: Side Stepping

1. *Stand at the bottom of a slope with your skis across the slope.*
2. *Press your knees into the slope—this will make the uphill edges of your skis bite into the snow and hold you from slipping back.*
3. *Keeping your skis parallel to each other, lift your uphill ski up one step. Lift the other ski up along side of the first. Imagine you are walking sideways up a staircase.*

There are other ways to climb a slope, but for beginners side stepping is the easiest.

Straight Running or Schussing

When you feel you are ready to take a straight run down the hill—called *Schussing*—start with a slight slope that finishes in a wide area where you have plenty of room to stop. Hopefully, there will be an upgrade—another small hill—at the bottom to help you slow down.

WHEN YOU'RE READY TO LEARN SCHUSSING
PRACTICE ON A GENTLE SLOPE.

Discovery

1. *Can you slide along in a straight line with your skis together down a slight hill?*
2. *How many different parts of your body can you bend as you ski down a gentle slope?*
3. *Can you move very lightly down a slope? Make believe you're floating?*
4. *Point your skis downhill to a spot you can reach by skiing. See how many ways you can balance yourself on skis as you ski to the spot (without falling).*

Game: Snowball

Directions: Find a very gentle slope with an easy runoff, and locate an object you can toss back and forth to a friend (for example, a glove, a hat, a piece of hard snow, an old tennis ball). Schuss down alongside of each other, throwing the object back and forth without dropping it.

Review: Straight Running/Schussing

1. *Without using poles, stand with your skis about shoulder-width apart.*
2. *Bend your knees slightly until your body is lowered and well balanced over your bindings.*
3. *Keep your back straight but not rigid.*
4. *Keep your rear end tucked in.*
5. *Try to keep your weight centered over the balls of your feet.*

Stopping: Wedge and Hockey Stop

Stopping can be accomplished slowly and gradually using a wedge stop, or suddenly and completely with a hockey or jump stop.

Discovery

1. *From the top of a very small slope, push off just hard enough to begin moving slowly forward. Stop however you feel most comfortable.*
2. *Ski down from the top of a gentle slope, change direction, and stop as fast as you can without falling. What part of your body absorbed the force of the stop?*
3. *Ski down a gentle slope and make your skis form the shape of a pie slice. What happens?*
4. *Ski down a hill with your legs apart, and see if you can apply a light, strong force to the inside of your knees using only your lower body. Can you? What does it feel like?*

Game: Stop Tag

Directions: Find a gentle hill. Like any game of tag, one person is "it" and tries to tag another to make that person "it." Moving skiers can be tagged; skiers who have stopped completely are safe. The object is to ski down the slope without being tagged.

Review: Stopping

No doubt you have found out quickly that stopping is sometimes a bit of a problem. Let's go over the two basic stops.

HOCKEY STOP. This is the best way of stopping because it stops you quickly and it is related to parallel skiing technique, which I think all skiers should learn.

1. *As you are skiing down a gentle slope, sink down by pushing the top part of your lower leg into the top part of your boot.*
2. *As you do this, keep the upper part of your body (above the waist) straight.*
3. *Come back up with a quick upward spring, turn your skis across the hill, and dig the uphill edges of your skies into the snow.*
4. *Keep your head and arms facing downhill.*
5. *To help keep your arms in the correct position, imagine you are carrying a tray of food. This will help you keep your weight over the downhill ski, which is important.*
6. *At first, try turning in the direction you feel most comfortable (almost every skier favors one side), but very soon try the other side, too. You must practice turning and stopping in both directions.*

HOCKEY STOP.

35

MAKING A WEDGE (OR PIE SLICE) WITH
YOUR SKIS IS A GOOD WAY TO CONTROL SPEED
OR TO STOP.

WEDGE STOP. This is another, more gradual method of stopping.

1. *Find a gentle slope that will not give you too much speed. Put your skis in the pie-slice (or inverted V) position by pushing your knees inward as you glide down the slope.*
2. *Put more pressure on the inside of your knees by making the V wider. This puts pressure on the inside of your ski edges, which forces you to lose speed.*

Turning

Turning controls both your direction and speed as you come down a hill. If you aren't controlling your speed at this point in your progress as a skier, some bad things and one good thing will happen to you. The bad things are all the falls you'll take. The good thing is that you'll become an expert at getting up off the snow.

Discovery

1. *How many ways can you make yourself tall and short on your skis as you make a curved path down the hill?*
2. *How many times can you jump first to the right side, then to the left, as you ski down a gentle slope?*
3. *Try skiing down the hill with your skis slightly apart, and apply a light force to the inside of your skis using only your lower body to apply the force. What happens?*
4. *Can you make a smooth, curving path first to one side, then to the other as you ski down the hill?*
5. *How smoothly can you make your up and down movements as you move forward on your skis?*
6. *Find the most comfortable position while you move forward on your skis. Is most of your weight in front of or in the back of your feet?*

37

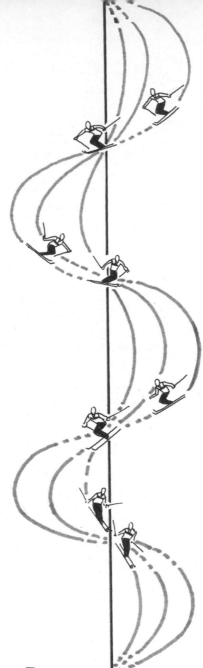

Game: Slalom Race

Directions: Set up two or three ski poles some distance apart on an easy slope. Make believe you are having a race, and try to ski around the poles as quickly as you can without falling. As you improve, add more poles to ski around.

38

Review: Turning

Now that you have some feeling for the different forces to use in turning your skis, it's a good idea to begin learning turns by doing exaggerated hops as you ski. By gradually making the hops smaller and smaller, you will learn parallel-turning skills.

HOP TURN: Imagine that your lower body is like a ball.

1. *Find a very easy slope and start down in a schuss.*
2. *Just like a bouncing ball, drop down by doing a deep knee bend with your legs. Keep facing downhill with your upper body.*
3. *Bounce back up by quickly straightening your legs. As you do this, remember to come forward over your skis—do not push your upper body backward as you rise up. If you push backward as you bounce up, you'll lose control of your skis.*
4. *Keep your arms in front of you to help you keep your weight forward.*
5. *Keep your skis as close together as feels comfortable.*
6. *Keep your weight on the balls of your feet, not back on your heels.*

5

Getting Better

When you were practicing straight running (schussing), stopping, and turning, you were advised to stay on gentle slopes. Now, however, you have learned the basic skills and are ready to use them in different ways to become a more advanced skier. You are ready to try longer, steeper hills. To ski the tougher slopes you have to do more things with your turning to control your speed and direction exactly.

Traversing

When you ski across a slope—rather than straight down it—you are doing a traverse. If you watched the path a good skier carved while skiing down a steep slope, it would look like a continuous series of S's. The better the skier, the smaller the S figures in the snow. This is because a better skier makes quicker, shorter turns in and out of the traverse positions. A less experienced skier needs to traverse a steep slope longer and more gradually to control the speed.

Try skiing a steeper slope. Look across the hill at a spot you wish to reach. Start your traverse so that you can reach that spot. When you do, look for another spot on the other side of the hill, a little further down than the first, and turn and begin traversing toward it.

Discovery

1. *As you are traversing the hill, how many different shapes can you make with your skis in the snow and still stay in balance?*
2. *How many different ways can you lean your body over your skis as you traverse?*
3. *Leaning downhill, how wide can you keep your skis apart? How close can you keep your skis together?*
4. *Look downhill as your knees and arms lead you across the slope, and notice where most of your weight seems to be pressing down. Is most of your weight on your uphill ski or on your downhill ski?*
5. *Can you travel across the hill with your knees bent slightly over your bindings, making believe you are carrying a tray of glasses while you are facing downhill?*

SKIING A TRAVERSE.

Game: Follow the Leader

Directions: Do this with a friend. Take turns being the leader. The leader traverses the hill, doing some of the exploration activities listed previously. The follower does everything the leader does.

Review: Traverse

While exploring the traverse skills, you have started to discover some of the advanced skills you will need to become an intermediate skier. These are:

1. **SLIDING,** *a flattening of the bottom of the skis so that they slip sideways down the hill.*
2. **EDGING,** *the pressing of both knees into the hill so that the edges of the skis bite into the snow.*
3. **CARVING,** *a turn that uses the edging of the skis to control the turning motion and that allows very little sideways sliding or skidding.*

A skier who skids when turning (the skis slide on the snow when coming around) loses speed when turning. A skier who carves turns (the skis bite firmly into the snow) loses very little speed while changing direction. Thus racers and advanced skiers strive for carved turns. Novice and intermediate skiers, however, often appreciate the speed control a sliding turn gives on steep slopes.

If you have successfully explored the different parts of traversing, your body position should be similar to this:

1. *Skis together—perhaps shoulder width apart—pointing across the slope.*
2. *Uphill ski slightly in front of the downhill ski.*
3. *Weight centered over your downhill ski.*
4. *Your upper body facing downhill.*
5. *Knees slightly bent and slightly rotated uphill.*
6. *Your arms out in front of you (holding the make-believe tray).*

As you practice all the skills we have talked about here, you will find that your S turns down the slope will gradually get smaller and smaller. Then try a steeper slope and start working on making your big S turns into smaller S turns again. Eventually, if you keep at it, there won't be a slope you can't ski—it will just be a matter of how big you will have to make your S turns. However, don't try steep slopes too quickly. Don't take chances skiing beyond your ability.

Poles

The only thing a beginner needs ski poles for is ease in moving along flat areas. Ski poles can be dangerous if used incorrectly. You should never try to stop yourself with your poles. Stand at the bottom of a slope, and watch a beginning skier ski down. What is he or she doing with the poles? Probably swinging them around wildly, as this is a common problem.

The correct use of poles in turning is to begin the turn by planting the tip of the pole to the side toward which you are going. Planting the pole to start a turn becomes more precise as you improve your skiing ability.

USE OF POLES PREPARING FOR TURN.

6

What's Ahead

It is good to read as much as possible about skiing. Here are some suggestions for books and other publications that can teach you more.

SKI Magazine
380 Madison Avenue
New York, NY 10017
7 issues/subscription: $7.90
SKIING Magazine
1 Park Avenue
New York, NY 10016
7 issues/subscription: $7
POWDER Magazine
Surfer Publications, Inc.
Box 1028
Dana Point, Calif. 92629
7 issues/subscription: $8

BOOKS
Ski Magazine's Complete Book of Ski Technique
Harper & Row Co.
New York, 1975
The Skier's Bible
Morten Lund
Doubleday, New York
1980 (updated edition)
We Learned to Ski
Evans, Jackman and Ottaway
St. Martin's Press, New York
1975

Ski With the Big Boys
Stu Campbell
Winchester Press, New York
1974
Inner Skiing
Tim Gallwey and Bob Kriegal
Random House, New York
1977
Inside Skiing
Phil Byrne
Nelson-Hall Inc., Chicago
1979
The Skier's Almanac
I. William Berry
Charles Scribner's Sons, New York
1979

ORGANIZATIONS
United States Ski Association (USSA)
1726 Champa
Suite 300
Denver, Colo. 80202
(In charge of amateur competition in the U.S. through regional divisions, up to and including the U.S. Ski Team)

NASTAR (National Standard Race)
P.O. Box 4500
Aspen, Colo. 81611
(Runs amateur races for beginner to advanced skiers through local areas—95 areas across the U.S. in 1980.)
Equitable Family Challenge
Capital Sports
280 Park Avenue
New York, NY 10017
(Runs family ski competitions at various local areas)
National Ski Areas Association (NSAA)
20 Maple Street
Springfield, Mass. 01101
(Organization of local ski areas in the U.S.)
National Ski Patrol System, Inc.
2901 Sheridan Boulevard
Denver, Colo. 80214
(Organization of volunteer ski patrollers.)
Professional Ski Instructors of America (PSIA)
2015 South Pontiac Way
Suite 1A
Denver, Colo. 80224
(Organization of certified ski instructors.)

SKI AREAS
Your local ski shop certainly has information about the best ski areas closest to where you live. Here is a sample list of good areas noted for quality instructional programs.

Alaska
Mt. Alyeska Ski Area
Girdwood, Alaska 99587

Arizona
Sunrise Ski Area
McNary, Arizona 85930

California
Mammoth Mt. Ski Area
P.O. Box 24
Mammoth Lakes, Calif. 93546

Squaw Valley Ski Area
P.O. Box 2007
Olympic Valley, Calif. 95730

Colorado
Aspen Buttermilk Ski Area
Box 4546
Apsen, Colo. 81611

Copper Mountain Ski Area
P.O. Box 3
Cooper Mt. Colo. 80443
(Member: SKIwee, special
children's program.)

Winter Park Ski Area
Winter Park, Colo. 80482
(Member: SKIwee, special
children's program.)

Connecticut
Mohawk Ski Area
Cornwall, Conn.

Idaho
Sun Valley Ski Area
Sun Valley, Idaho 83353

Maine
Sugarloaf/USA
Kingfield, Maine 04947
(Member: SKIwee, special
children's program.)

Maryland
Wisp Ski Area
Oakland, Maryland

Massachusetts
Butternut Basin
P.O. Box 347
Great Barrington, Mass. 01230
(Member: SKIwee, special
children's program.)

Jiminy Peak Ski Area
Hancock, Mass. 02137

Michigan
Big Powderhorn Ski Area
Box 136
Bessemer, Mich. 44911

Minnesota
Lutsen Ski Area
Lutsen, Minnesota 55617

Montana
Big Ski Ski Area
Big Sky, Mont. 59716

Nevada
Ski Incline
P.O. Box AL
Incline Village, Nev. 89450

New Hampshire
Wildcat Mountain
Pinkham Notch
Jackson, N.H. 03846
(Member: SKIwee, special
children's program.)

Waterville Valley
Waterville Co., Inc.
Waterville Valley, N.H. 03223
(Member: SKIwee, special
children's program.)

New Jersey
Vernon Valley/Great Gorge
Box 848
McAfee, New Jersey 07428

New Mexico
Taos Ski Valley
Taos, N.M. 87571

New York
Hunter Mountain Ski Bowl
Hunter, N.Y. 12442

North Carolina
Ski Beech
Box 118
Banner Elk, N.C. 28604
(Member: SKIwee, special
children's program.)

Oregon
Timberline
Timberline Lodge
Government Camp, Oregon 97028

Pennsylvania
Camelback Ski Area
Tannersville, Pa. 18372

South Dakota
Great Bear Ski Valley
Sioux Falls, S.D.

Utah
Park City Ski Area
Box 39
Park City, Utah 84060

Sundance Ski Area
P.O. Box 837
Provo, Utah 84403

Vermont
Bromley Ski Area
Manchester, Vt. 05255

Killington Ski Area
Killington, Vt. 05751

Mt. Snow Ski Area
Mount Snow, Vt. 05356
(Member: SKIwee, special
children's program.)

Stratton Mt. Ski Area
Stratton Mountain, Vt. 05155

Washington
Northshore Ski School
8206 N.E. 117th Street
Kirkland, Washington 98033
(Member: SKIwee, special
children's program.)

Mt. Baker Ski Area
2014 Moore St.
Bellingham, Wash. 98225

West Virginia
Snowshoe Ski Area
Slaty Fork, W.V. 26291

Wisconsin
Mt. Telemark
Cable, Wis. 54821

Wyoming
Jackson Hole
Teton Village, Wyo. 83025
(Member: SKIwee, special
children's program.)

Canada
Mont Tremblant Ski Area
Mont Tremblant, Quebec JOT-120

Whistler Mt. Ski Area
Alta Lake, British Columbia

Now that you have read all the foregoing pages, perhaps have been out on the snows and have a little practice you have discovered that there is much more to learn. Yes, there is.

You will want to learn how to ski the steeper hills, how to bounce off the "bumps" and how to make the fancy quick, tight turns down the hill. Ask you local ski school director for guidance and instruction for this advanced type of skiing.

OK, then! You're off! Have the time of your life, I look forward to seeing you on the hills.

INDEX